QUEEN VICTORIA

WHO WAS...

QUEEN VICTORIA

The Woman Who Ruled the World

KATE HUBBARD

✱ SHORT BOOKS

Published in 2004 by
Short Books
15 Highbury Terrace
London N5 1UP

10 9 8 7 6 5 4 3 2

Text Copyright ©
Kate Hubbard 2004

A CIP catalogue record for this book
is available from the British Library.

ISBN 1-904095-82-8

Printed in Great Britain by
Bookmarque Ltd, Croydon, Surrey

'GOD SAVE THE QUEEN'

June 22nd 1897. A beautiful day. 'Queen's weather' it was called. The streets of London decked with flowers and heaving with people. Thousands squeezed into wooden stands built right up to the rooftops. Still more standing on the roofs themselves, or hanging out of windows. And there, coming into the Mall, a column of colonial troops. And behind them a carriage, pulled by eight horses, bearing a very stout little old lady, in a black and grey dress and a bonnet. Queen Victoria. Her Diamond Jubilee.

As she drove past the wildly cheering crowds, smiling and jauntily swinging her parasol, Victoria looked back, 60 years before, to the 18-year-old girl in her night-gown, woken by her mother to be told that she was Queen. It felt like another life. It *was* another life. For 60 years had seen Britain quite transformed. Long gone were the days of sputtering gas lamps and stinking cesspools. Now people enjoyed electric light, sewers, gramophones, bicycles, motor cars, typewriters and telephones. Victoria didn't necessarily think much of these new inventions – she hadn't felt a bit safe on a tricycle; cars were dreadfully smelly and shaky. Still, she had to admit it was progress and certainly Britain had never been so rich and powerful or the British Empire more glorious.

Before leaving Buckingham Palace, the Queen had touched an electric button and telegraphed (that would have been unthinkable in 1837) her Jubilee message around the Empire – 'From my heart I thank my beloved people. May God bless them!' As her carriage pulled up at the steps of St Paul's, her people tossed their hats in the air and broke into 'God Save the Queen'. And tears rolled down Her Majesty's soft, sagging cheeks.

CHAPTER ONE

B ack in 1817 the British monarchy had a crisis on its hands. For the past 100 years Britain had been ruled by overweight Germans (from Hanover) – George I, George II and, now, George III. These Hanoverian Kings tended to be stubborn, hot-tempered, indolent and more interested, or so it seemed to their subjects, in Germany, than in Britain. George III was actually a good deal more popular than his predecessors, but sadly he had gone stark, staring mad and so his son, the Prince of Wales, had been made Prince Regent, which allowed him to take over his father's royal duties.

The Prince Regent was a painted and perfumed dandy, so grossly fat that they called him the 'Prince of Whales' behind his back. He had married an ugly German princess, Caroline of Brunswick, and, though he detested her, they had managed to produce a single child, Princess Charlotte, the heir to the throne. In 1816 Charlotte married Prince Leopold of Saxe-Coburg. But just a year later she was dead, having given birth to a still-born son.

Where was the heir to the throne now? The Prince Regent was in poor health and separated from his wife. George III's remaining six sons, the Dukes of York, Clarence, Kent, Cumberland, Sussex and Cambridge, were a sorry lot with not a legitimate child, though a good many illegitimate, between them (the King's five daughters were either childless or spinsters). Only the Duke of York and the Duke of Cumberland were married at all. The Duke of York couldn't stand the sight of his wife, while the Duke of Cumberland, with his horribly scarred face and his portfolio of vices, was married to a woman who was rumoured to be a murderess. It was the patriotic duty of the bachelor brothers to marry and produce heirs. The race was on.

The Duke of Kent was George III's fourth son. He had lived very happily for 27 years with a woman who was not his wife called Madame de St Laurent. They had moved to Brussels (the Duke was always in debt and Brussels was cheap). Here, one morning in 1817, Madame de St Laurent sat down to breakfast, opened the newspaper and gave a little scream. She saw that Princess Charlotte had died. She read the report calling on the royal dukes to marry. Madame de St Laurent wept; she knew her days were numbered.

The Duke of Kent knew his duty – his mistress must pack her bags and make way for a suitable bride. He found her in the person of Victoria of Saxe-Coburg, a German princess (there was always a German princess), whose brother Leopold had been married to Princess Charlotte. Victoria was a 30-year-old-widow with two children, rather plump, moderately attractive, warm-hearted and unable to speak a word of English. She and the Duke became very fond of each other.

The newly married Duke and Duchess of Kent couldn't afford to live in England, so they took themselves off to the Duchess's home, a castle hidden deep in the forest near Amorbach, Germany. As dawn broke darkly on March 24th 1819 a cavalcade of carriages passed through the gates of the castle. Lap-dogs and songbirds, swinging in their cages, could be seen in one. Another carried a midwife and a lady's maid, a third a couple of cooks, while in a fourth carriage a man-servant rattled along with the royal plate. But leading the rest was a phaeton driven by the tall, portly figure of the Duke and bearing his heavily pregnant wife. The baby, the Duke had determined, must be born on English soil. After all there was a chance that the child might one day be King – or Queen.

Three weeks later the Duke's party rolled into the French port of Calais and from there they set sail for Dover. On May 24th, in apartments at Kensington Palace provided, most reluctantly, by the Prince Regent, the Duchess of Kent gave birth to a daughter, a fine healthy baby, as 'plump as a partridge'.

The Prince Regent, who disliked his brother and who, with no heir of his own, became quite apoplectic at the mere mention of his baby niece, decreed that the christening was to be private with absolutely no pomp or dressing up. So, on June 24th at Kensington Palace, in a room hung with crimson velvet, a small group gathered round the silver-gilt font that had been brought in from the Tower of London. The Archbishop of Canterbury held the baby. On one side of him stood the baby's parents and, on the other, her uncle, the Prince Regent. The Duke of Kent looked proud, the Duchess anxious and the Prince Regent bored and bad-tempered.

The names proposed for the baby by her parents were Georgiana Charlotte Augusta Alexandrina Victoria, but nobody had told the Archbishop. He looked hopefully towards the Prince Regent, who was godfather – 'And the child's names?' he asked. The Prince Regent, squeezed into his frock coat and breeches, with two spots of rouge on his cheeks and a powdered wig, remained silent.

'Georgiana,' prompted the Duke of Kent, only to be interrupted by the Prince Regent with a thunderous 'NO'.

'Charlotte', continued the Duke.

'On no account,' said his brother.

'Augusta,' tried the Duke. The Prince Regent shook his head vigorously, frosting his shoulders with powder, whereupon the Duchess of Kent burst into tears. The Prince Regent sighed. 'Let her be called after her mother,' he said brusquely, 'but the Tsar's name must come first' (as a mark of respect to Alexander I, Tsar of Russia, who was also a godfather).

And so it came to be that the baby was named Alexandrina Victoria. For the first nine years of her life she was known as 'Drina', and after that 'Victoria', the name she would give to over 60 years of British history.

CHAPTER TWO

The Duke of Kent was extremely proud of his 'pocket Hercules', as he called Victoria (the Duchess insisted on breast-feeding the baby herself, which was almost unheard of among aristocratic women in the 19th century). He was quite convinced that she would one day be Queen. The Christmas of 1819 he decided to take his family to Sidmouth in Devon for some bracing sea air. But, a few weeks later, having caught a chill while visiting Salisbury cathedral, he died of pneumonia. The Duchess of Kent was left with an eight-month-old baby and a pile of debts. She even had to borrow money to get back to London. On January 29th George III also died and the Prince Regent became George IV.

The Duchess and her daughter, her 'Vickelchen',

continued to live in their Kensington Palace apartments. For Victoria it was a simple, sheltered life, not at all what you might expect for a princess. The palace was very shabby and the meals very plain. It was mutton for lunch, and bread and milk for supper. *Every day.* Victoria never had her own room and instead slept in her mother's.

She had a nurse, Mrs Brock, who helped her dress every morning. This was a long and laborious business – first came combinations (long-sleeved, long-legged underwear, with buttons), then woollen stockings, then cotton drawers with more buttons, then petticoats, and then the blouse, and the collar and the pinafore and the button-boots. It seemed to last for ever and Victoria would sigh and squirm. Sometimes Mrs Brock pinned a sprig of holly to the front of her dress to encourage her to keep her chin up (left to itself Victoria's chin sloped gently backwards).

The princess's first words were not English, but German, the language that her mother spoke, the language that she heard around her (not until she was three did she start learning English). Her governess, Baroness Lehzen, was also German. The Baroness was a handsome, clever woman, with a long, tapering nose. There hung about her the whiff of caraway seeds, which she chewed constantly for her indigestion. She was absolutely devoted to Victoria, as Victoria was to her.

Lessons were supervised by a clergyman, the Rev. George Davys. In the mornings the princess had geography, history, arithmetic and drawing. After lunch came English, French and German. On Wednesday afternoon it was scripture, while Thursday and Friday mornings were taken up with dancing and music. Victoria didn't enjoy her lessons much, nor was she especially good at them. But she did have a very good memory and she drew, danced and sang extremely well.

But looming over Victoria's childhood was the hateful Sir John Conroy. Conroy had been on the staff of the Duke of Kent and after the Duke's death the Duchess had naturally turned to him for help and advice. She was short of money, hardly spoke any English and felt friendless in a country that wasn't her own. Putting all her trust in Conroy, she appointed him to manage her affairs and run her household. He soon had her eating out of his hand.

Handsome, scheming and ambitious, Conroy craved power – he had it over the Duchess and he wanted it over the princess. He was responsible for a regime that became known as the 'Kensington System'. This was intended to make Victoria completely dependent on her mother and, through her mother, on Conroy. He insisted that the princess be constantly supervised, that Lehzen be with her at all times and that she be shielded from unsuitable outside influences. He also encouraged the Duchess's fears that the Duke of Cumberland (next in line for the throne after Victoria) was plotting to have his niece kidnapped or poisoned. Kensington Palace became a little kingdom, cut off from the court and ruled over by Conroy.

When she grew up, Victoria would remember her childhood as lonely and 'rather melancholy'. There were treats – visits to the opera and the ballet, which Victoria loved, and opportunities for dancing, which she loved even more. But she spent a good many hours gazing out through the windows at Kensington Gardens, longing for some companions of her own age. She had her half-sister Feodore, whom she adored, but Feodore was 12 years older, too old to play with. There was also Conroy's daughter Victoire, but naturally she hated her. Victoria knew her mother loved her, but she never listened to her, only to Conroy; sometimes they even seemed to be *flirting*. It was too revolting.

For company Victoria resorted to the 132 wooden dolls for whom she'd made costumes and given names and characters. She had Lehzen of course – 'my ANGELIC dearest mother Lehzen whom I do so adore' – and her spaniel, Dash, whom she dressed up in a scarlet jacket and blue trousers. And every Wednesday afternoon her beloved uncle Leopold would visit, tottering on three-inch heels and swathed in a feather boa. Those visits, however, came to an end when Leopold became King of Belgium.

Like a great many children in the 19th century, Victoria was brought up to be virtuous, dutiful and pious. She was encouraged to keep a Behaviour Book. One entry read '*very, very, very, terribly naughty*'. For, however good her intentions, she was headstrong, wilful and quick-tempered. Was she going to allow herself to be bossed? No, she was not. When she didn't get her way there were terrible tantrums. After one such tantrum the Duchess of Kent said, 'When you are naughty you make yourself very unhappy.' 'No, mama, not me, not myself, but you,' corrected her daughter. Her piano teacher once remarked, 'There is no royal road to success in music, Princess Victoria, you must practise you know.' Victoria slammed down the lid and declared, 'There! You see there is no must about it.' On another occasion she threw a pair of scissors at Lehzen.

From the seclusion of Kensington Palace, the court seemed a distant place to Victoria, though she'd heard plenty of tales of her 'wicked uncles' – George IV and the royal dukes. So it was quite an event when, in the summer of 1826, the seven-year-old princess was taken by her mother to Windsor Castle, to see her 'Uncle King'. George IV had never looked particularly kindly on his niece, but the sight of the small figure with her round blue eyes looking up from under her bonnet softened his heart and he bent down to her saying, 'Give me your little paw.' Then she found herself hoisted onto the royal knee for a kiss, which was 'too disgusting because his face was covered with grease paint'.

The next day she was walking in the park with her

mother when the King came bowling along in his phaeton (an open carriage). He stopped, crying 'Pop her in!' and Victoria found herself whirled away, squashed between her uncle and one of her royal aunts. When the time came to leave the King enquired, 'Tell me what you enjoyed most about your visit?' and she replied, 'The drive with you.' She could be tactful when she wanted to.

When Victoria was 11, Lehzen placed a family tree in one of her history books. It showed that after George IV and the Duke of Clarence, Victoria was next in line for the throne. It was the first time she understood that her destiny was not that of ordinary children. 'I am nearer to the throne than I thought,' she cried and burst into tears. Then she lifted her chin and declared, 'I will be good.' From that day on Victoria had a strong sense of duty. The prospect of becoming queen was indeed overwhelming, but if it came to be, she would be a good queen, a great queen.

By the spring of 1830 it was clear that time was running out for George IV. His legs were so swollen that he could no longer walk, his heart was weak, he was going blind and, unable to lie down, he spent his nights uncomfortably propped in an armchair. On June 26th he died and the Duke of Clarence became King William IV. For Victoria the throne was just a step away.

William IV was a kindly man, although he looked more like a bumbling country gentleman than a king. He had a habit of spitting out of the windows of his coach and he was often to be found wandering the streets of London chatting to passers-by. He and his wife, Queen Adelaide, had four children, all of whom died as babies. They were both fond of Victoria, who now everyone acknowledged as heir to the throne. But the King disliked the Duchess of Kent, who strongly disapproved of his moving his ten illegitimate children into Windsor Castle. He disliked Conroy and he particularly disliked the 'royal progresses' that Conroy organised for Victoria.

These were tours around the country, to show off the princess to the people of England. In 1832, when Victoria was 13, she embarked on the first of these 'progresses', travelling around the Midlands. This was one of the few occasions she actually came face to face with the terrible poverty suffered by so many in 19th-century Britain. She described her shock at the sight of the 'desolate' coal-mining country – the roaring furnaces, the blackened landscape, the 'ragged children'.

It was now that Victoria began to write a diary, which she would keep every day for the rest of her life. On May 24th 1833 she wrote, 'Today is my birthday. I am today fourteen years old! How very old!' The King and Queen gave a ball for her and she danced quadrilles till 12.30 at night.

In 1835, while staying at Ramsgate, Victoria became seriously ill. It may have been typhoid, a disease that was often fatal in the 19th century. She recovered, but while she was still thin and weak and just beginning to eat the odd spoonful of orange jelly, Conroy tried to persuade her to sign a paper promising him the position of private secretary when she became queen. Victoria refused. How dare he take advantage of her weakness in this way! She wouldn't listen to Conroy's arguments, or her mother's pleas. Her only ally, she felt, was Lehzen.

CHAPTER THREE

Two years later, at six a.m on June 20th 1837, the Duchess of Kent woke her daughter with the news that King William IV had died. At 18 years old Victoria found herself Queen of the United Kingdom of Great Britain and Ireland. She burst into tears. 'I shall do my utmost to fulfil my duty towards my country,' she wrote in her diary, 'I am very young and perhaps in many, though not in all things, inexperienced, but I am sure that very few have more real goodwill and more real desire to do what is fit and right than I have.'

That same morning the new Queen had an audience with her Prime Minister, Lord Melbourne, and held her first Privy Council (a group of politicians and notable personages who advised the monarch) in Kensington Palace. As the long line of Councillors knelt to kiss her hand and swear allegiance, they were struck by the tiny figure – Victoria was under five foot tall – blushing yet composed, modest yet regal. It was also noticed how, the moment she was out of the door, Victoria skipped away, rubbing her hands. During the next few hours she saw Lord Melbourne again, then the Archbishop of Canterbury; she appointed a court physician; she wrote a letter to her uncle Leopold; and she dismissed Conroy. In a voice as clear and silvery as a bell she told Baroness Lehzen – 'Kindly see to it that my bed is removed from Mama's room.' The schoolgirl had become a queen.

In some ways, though, she was still a schoolgirl – she loved playing shuttlecock in the corridors of Windsor with her ladies and staying up late, she gobbled her food and laughed a lot with her mouth wide open, showing pink gums. But, as queen, she was determined to assert herself. She immediately set about paying off her father's debts, because she felt it her duty to do so. When her mother and Melbourne suggested it wasn't proper to review her troops on horseback, Victoria cried, 'Nonsense!' and, with a toss of her head, insist-ed on riding her horse. Mama, in fact, found herself put firmly in her place. She had to ask for permission to see her daughter and quite often a note came back with a single word – 'Busy'.

Victoria held very decided opinions. She drew up a list of things she simply loathed the thought of – turtle soup, insects, dying young, going blind and Tories. And the things she loved? Cream cakes and trifle, a glass (or two) of ale, dancing, riding and her spaniel Dash. In May 1838 she gave her first State Ball and stayed up dancing till four a.m. And on June 28th she was crowned.

The Coronation sent the whole of London into a fever of excitement. People stayed up all night, or camped in the park. Victoria was woken at four a.m. by the sound of a gun salute and at seven she was dressed in robes of crimson velvet edged with ermine. She rode to Westminster Abbey in the golden state coach, smiling and bowing to every side. The sight of the ecstatic crowds was quite overwhelming – 'I really cannot say how proud I feel to be the Queen of *such a Nation,*' she wrote. On their part, her subjects had taken her to their hearts. No one had loved the last three kings – the one a madman, the other a dandy and the third a fool. People had grown sick of being ruled by bloated

Germans with mistresses and illegitimate children and debts. How different was this girl-Queen, as pure and fresh as a dewdrop. Here was Youth, Innocence and Duty. Here was a Queen who behaved like a Queen.

Inside the Abbey Victoria proceeded slowly up the aisle, a doll-sized figure amid a blur of faces and a dazzle of scarlet and gold. Behind her stumbled her train-bearers, wearing white satin dresses and wreaths of silver corn-ears. The coronation ceremony was extremely long and elaborate and nobody seemed to understand it. The various bishops made various muddles. The Bishop of Durham lost his place in the prayer book. The Archbishop of Canterbury forced the ruby ring onto the wrong finger, which made it extremely painful for Victoria to take off later. 'Pray tell me what to do for they don't know!' Victoria begged a court official at one point. There was another mishap when the elderly Lord Rolle, approaching the throne to pay homage, lived up to his name and rolled down the steps. Everybody noticed how the Queen instantly rose to her feet and bent down to help him.

At the moment of crowning, a gleaming wave of gold swept the Abbey as the peers and peeresses put on their coronets, while trumpets sounded and guns boomed. It was a whole five hours, throughout which Victoria remained absolutely composed and dignified, before she got back into the coach, wearing her crown and struggling to carry the heavy orb and sceptre, and rode back to the palace. The minute she was through the door she ran straight upstairs to give Dash his bath.

The summer of 1838, Victoria wrote, was the 'pleasantest summer she had EVER passed in her life'. But, with all the pomp and ceremony over, it was necessary to apply herself to the business of being Queen, which she did most conscientiously. Every day she was presented with dispatch boxes full of papers to read and documents to sign. This was made much less daunting by the presence of her Prime Minister, Lord Melbourne ('Lord M'), who soon became absolutely indispensable. He came to see her in the morning; they rode together in the afternoon; he dined at the palace. Melbourne was leader of the Whig party (the Whigs stood for such causes as liberty and toleration, in moderation of course; later in the century they were replaced by a new party, the Liberals). At the beginning of her reign, Victoria was fiercely loyal to the Whigs, and to Melbourne in particular, though of course as queen she wasn't meant to take sides in political matters.

At 58 years old, Melbourne was a man of the world – witty, sophisticated and cynical. He did his best not to take anything too seriously and Victoria found his conversation delightfully scandalous. She looked up to him as to a wise father, but he also made her laugh.

But Victoria's popularity was not to be taken for granted, as she discovered in 1839, thanks to a scandal known as the Hastings affair. Lady Flora Hastings was a lady-in-waiting to the Duchess of Kent. It was noticed that Lady Flora's stomach was strangely swollen. There were whisperings in the corridors – could she possibly be pregnant? As she was unmarried, this was a shocking state of affairs. The Queen had never liked Lady Flora – a 'detestable person' she said – and was quite ready to believe that she was indeed pregnant, and furthermore that Sir John Conroy, 'the Monster and Demon Incarnate', was the father. Lord Melbourne and Baroness Lehzen, the two people she most trusted, were of the same opinion. But after Lady Flora had reluctantly agreed to be examined by the royal doctor it was declared that she wasn't pregnant at all.

Yet there still remained the swollen stomach; the whispering continued and the Queen did nothing to stop it. Lady Flora's family were furious and she herself was now seriously ill. In fact she was said to be dying, though Victoria refused to believe it. When, however, she finally consented to visit the invalid she was deeply shocked to find her 'literally a skeleton'. A week later the 'skeleton' was just that: dead. A post mortem revealed that Lady Flora had been suffering from a tumour. Reports appeared in the press criticising the Queen's behaviour and she was hissed in the streets of London. The Queen claimed she felt no remorse, but for the first time she realised how easily public opinion could turn against her. It made her feel alone.

She felt even more so when, in May 1839, the Whig government fell and the Queen had to call on Sir Robert Peel, the leader of the opposition party, the Tories, to form a new government. How could Victoria possibly do without her beloved Lord M? 'I am but a poor helpless girl who clings to him for support and protection and the thought of ALL ALL my happiness being possibly at stake so completely overcame me that

I burst into tears and remained crying for some time,' she wrote in her diary. How could she have cosy chats with Peel, so cold and formal?

The poor helpless girl decided to show what she was made of. When Peel came for an audience, and asked her if she would be willing to replace some of her Ladies of the Bedchamber who were married to Whig ministers with Ladies married to Tories (this was so the Queen wouldn't appear to favour the Whigs), Victoria saw her chance.

'Now, Ma'am, about your ladies,' Peel began, nervously, – 'Do you intend to retain all of them?'

'All,' came the answer.

'Even the most senior?' he persisted.

'All.'

Peel retreated, at a loss, and the Queen wrote to Melbourne – 'I was very calm but very decided... the Queen of England will not submit to such trickery. Keep yourself in readiness for you may soon be wanted.'

The great Duke of Wellington, the hero of the Battle of Waterloo (where Napoleon was defeated), was called in to bring his influence to bear. He bowed stiffly before the Queen, and said – 'Well, I am sorry to find there is a difficulty.'

'Oh, Sir Robert began it not me,' replied Victoria airily, 'Anyway, he should know I never talk politics with my ladies.'

Wellington gave up. Peel declared that if the Queen was not willing to show confidence in the Tory party by replacing some of her ladies, he could not form a government. Victoria had won. The Whigs returned and Lord M was by her side once more.

CHAPTER FOUR

It was necessary for the Queen to marry, as she well knew, and what's more to marry suitably. But she was in no hurry. She was only 20 and, with the difficult summer of 1839 over, she was greatly enjoying herself.

How delightful it was to be whirled around in the arms of the handsome Grand Duke Alexander of Russia (son and heir of the Tsar) till 2 a.m. at a ball at Buckingham Palace. How she looked forward to her cosy tête-à-têtes with Lord M. How pleasant were the evenings of gossiping with her ladies and playing chess and whist. How charming to always have one's own way and no one to answer to. Surely marriage could wait. But, for several years, Victoria's uncle Leopold had been plotting a match with her German first cousin, Albert, the second son of the Duke of Saxe-

Coburg-Gotha, who was the eldest brother of Leopold and the Duchess of Kent.

Victoria had first met Albert when he and his brother Ernest had come to England three years earlier, to celebrate her 17th birthday, and she had thought him handsome and charming, though she was alarmed by his habit of nodding off early in the evening, just when the dancing was getting going. She agreed to a second visit, but only as long as it was understood that there was absolutely no engagement – she was simply going to get to know him a little better and see how she felt.

Lord Melbourne tried to put her off Germans – they all smoked, he said, and they never washed their faces. Victoria was more worried about the fact that Albert didn't speak perfect English. And Albert had his doubts about her. He had heard that his cousin was terribly stubborn, that she insisted on the strictest protocol at court and that she loved late nights and long mornings in bed. Albert was a serious young man. How could they get along?

On the evening of 10th October 1839 Albert and his brother Ernest arrived at Windsor. They had crossed the Channel in a terrible storm and Albert, whose health was always delicate, was looking distinctly green. To Victoria, however, standing at the top of the stairs to greet her cousins, he was a vision. She was smitten. Her world changed forever. 'Albert,' she wrote in her diary, 'is BEAUTIFUL.' His nose was 'exquisite', his mouth 'pretty', his moustachios and whiskers 'delicate', his figure, with his broad shoulders and fine waist, 'beautiful'. 'My heart is quite going,' she said, and suddenly marriage seemed a very good idea indeed. And the sooner the better.

A German prince could not presume to propose to an English queen. So on 15th October Victoria summoned Albert. Nervous as she was, she remembered the squeeze he had given her hand the night before and felt encouraged to speak. She told him that it would make her 'too happy' if he would consent to marry her. Albert took her hands and kissed them and, in a rush of German, declared that he longed to spend his life with her. They fell into each other's arms. That evening came a note – 'How is it that I have deserved so much love, so much affection? I believe that Heaven has sent me an angel... In body and soul ever your slave, your loyal ALBERT.'

The engaged couple were inseparable. They sang duets together, they walked and rode in the park, they exchanged rings and locks of hair and whispered endearments in German (they often spoke German in private). When Victoria reviewed the troops in Hyde Park, Albert went with her, wearing, she was thrilled to notice, a pair of white cashmere breeches with '*nothing under them*'. While she put her signature to state papers he sat beside her holding the blotting paper. And whenever they were alone together kisses fell like rain. This was no arranged marriage. She was marrying for love.

But, as Albert soon discovered, it was his wife who intended to wear the breeches in their marriage. Albert wished to choose his staff – known as his 'household' – himself. This was not acceptable. The Queen and Lord M chose Albert's Private Secretary for him and that was that, as the Queen explained – 'I am distressed to tell you what I fear you do not like, but it is necessary, my dearest, most excellent Albert. Once more I tell you that you can perfectly rely on me in these matters.' Albert's suggestion that perhaps their honeymoon could be a little longer than two or three days at

Windsor was firmly squashed – 'You forget, my dearest Love, that I am the Sovereign, and that business can stop and wait for nothing.'

Albert was leaving his home and coming to a country whose language, customs and people were unfamiliar to him. He was a highly intelligent young man, with a thorough knowledge of philosophy, the arts and science, yet was he never to do more than stand by with the blotting paper? It wasn't surprising that he felt somewhat anxious about his marriage. The Queen had no such reservations. She could hardly wait.

The wedding took place on February 10th 1840. In Buckingham Palace (Queen Victoria was the first monarch to live in Buckingham Palace), the Queen was helped into her gown of white satin, trimmed with Honiton lace, with a diamond necklace and a sapphire brooch, given to her by Albert. Her light-brown hair was parted in two smooth wings over her forehead, as was the fashion, and coiled over her ears. Victoria was not a beauty – her nose was slightly hooked, her blue eyes tended to bulge, she didn't have much in the way of a chin and already she was growing stout. But she had a charming smile, a beautiful voice and, if she lacked inches, every one of them was queenly.

She drove to the Chapel Royal at St James's through crowds who cheered their heads off at the sight of their Queen, her head bobbing beneath a wreath of orange blossoms, her diamonds twinkling in the sunlight (the sun always seemed to shine for state occasions – it became known as 'queen's weather'). At the chapel she was met by her 12 train-bearers and the ceremony began. Lord Melbourne watched with tears in his eyes.

After the wedding breakfast back at the palace, the Queen changed into a white silk dress trimmed with swansdown and a bonnet, before she and Albert drove off in their carriage for Windsor. They were accompanied by a large crowd of well-wishers, on horseback and in gigs. Then, at last, they were alone in their rooms and Albert put his Queen on his knee and, she wrote, it 'was bliss beyond belief'. Her head was aching so badly that she had to lie on the sofa 'but ill or not I NEVER NEVER spent such an evening!!! My DEAREST DEAREST DEAR Albert sat on a footstool by my side, and his excessive love and affection gave me feelings of heavenly love and happiness… how can I ever be thankful enough to have such a *Husband*!'

CHAPTER FIVE

The Queen floated in a haze of happiness – what a delight it was to sit and watch Albert shave every morning, how her heart fluttered at the sight of him in his tight breeches and scarlet boots. She was, however, extremely put out to discover that she was pregnant. Victoria liked children, but not babies, especially newly born when, she thought, they looked like frogs. An ugly baby was a 'very nasty object' and even the prettiest was 'frightful when undressed'. She certainly had no intention of breast-feeding. And she dreaded childbirth, which was a hazardous business in the 19th century, with women quite frequently dying. In case such a fate should befall the Queen, Albert was made Prince Regent, which meant he could take over her royal duties.

In November 1840, with Albert by her side and ministers and bishops hovering in the next door room, Victoria gave birth to a girl. 'Oh Madam, it is a princess,' said the doctor. 'Never mind, the next will be a prince,' replied the Queen briskly. A year later, she was proved right, when Bertie, the Prince of Wales, joined his sister Vicky, the Princess Royal, or 'Pussy', as her parents called her, in the royal nursery.

Childbirth wasn't the only danger the Queen faced. Driving out in her carriage one summer's day in 1840, she heard the crack of a pistol. Albert instantly flung his arms around her, pulling her down as another shot whistled over her head and the would-be assassin was seized by a passer-by. He was a simple-minded youth of 18, called Edward Oxford, and he was sent to an asylum for 27 years, though Victoria didn't believe he was the least bit mad and thought he should be hanged. When she was shown Oxford's pistols she remarked, with a shudder, that they 'might have *finished me off*'.

During her reign, the Queen would suffer no less than six more attacks, all by deranged youths. Once a mad midget fired a pistol full of tobacco and on another occasion a young man called Robert Pate leaned into her carriage, in front of her children, and gave her such a thwack on the head with his brass-ended walking stick that she was knocked unconscious for several seconds. That evening she went to the opera with a black eye and was loudly cheered – 'the lowest of the low being most indignant', she wrote.

And disturbed youths lurked inside the palace as well as out. One morning in December 1840 baby Vicky's nurse heard a scuffling under the sofa in the Queen's dressing-room and, bending down, saw a boy of 'most repulsive appearance' hiding there. It was 'The Boy Jones' who had already visited the Palace two years before when he'd gained entry disguised as a chimney sweep. This time he'd climbed over a wall and come in through a window. He claimed that he'd spent three days quite comfortably, hiding under beds and helping himself to soup and other delicacies. He said he'd sat on the Queen's throne and heard baby Vicky 'squall'. 'The Boy Jones' was sent to prison, but the minute he was released, he headed straight back to the Palace. Eventually he was sent to sea.

In September of 1841, when the Whig government was again defeated, the Queen lost Lord Melbourne for good. Sir Robert Peel became the new Prime Minister and there was nothing Victoria could do about it; not that this time she really wanted to. With Albert at her side she no longer needed Lord M, as she had done. 'I thought I was happy,' she wrote, of the days before her marriage, 'Thank God I now know what REAL happiness means!' In fact Victoria grew to trust Peel, partly for his good judgement, but also because he liked and respected Prince Albert.

The aristocracy, however, tended to look down their noses at Albert. They recognised his intelligence and good sense, they admitted that he danced well, played the organ beautifully and was even a passable shot on the hunting field. But he was so stiff, so humourless and above all so *German*. You could see it in the cut of his coat, his handshake, even the way he rode his horse. The ladies at court took offence when he showed no inclination to flirt with them – to be a devoted husband was one thing, but couldn't he pay the occasional compliment? It seemed he could not.

His wife and children, however, saw a different Albert. One who would play with the children for hours and was fond of jokes. When the Queen asked him how she could stop herself from looking grumpy during state occasions, he told her to behave like a ballet dancer and fix a smile on her face. He demonstrated by performing a perfect pirouette, grinning madly all the while, and ending with one foot pointed in the air.

In these early days of their marriage Albert still felt excluded from important affairs of state. He wrote sadly that he was 'the husband not the master of the house'. Gradually however his influence grew and the Queen came to rely on him more and more. He began to attend her meetings with her ministers, he gave advice and he drafted letters for her (though she had to check his English). Victoria was never so happy as when she and Albert sat at their desks, working side by side.

Yet there were also terrible scenes and shouting matches. 'Dearest Angel Albert' was perfection, yet he could be horribly aggravating. In fact the more reasonable, the more patient he was, the more aggravating Victoria found him. She was so easily upset – how could he remain so unruffled? They quarrelled over Lehzen, who was jealous of Albert and who Albert had never liked.

Albert blamed Lehzen for the fact that baby Vicky was sickly and not gaining weight. 'Our daughter is not growing as she should,' he complained to the Queen. 'Lehzen, ze nurse, ze doctor, zeh are all incompetent. Vat, may I ask, are you going to do about it?' Victoria instantly flew into a rage – 'You're trying to drive me out of my child's nursery!' she cried, 'If that's what you want, go ahead and murder your own daughter!' Muttering 'I must have patience,' Albert retired to his room to write a letter to his wife, as he often did when he couldn't reason with her.

Victoria, scarlet in the face and with tears popping hotly from her eyes, went after him and banged furiously on the locked door. 'Who is there?' he asked. 'The Queen of England!' came the imperious reply. The door remained locked. A hail of knocks followed. 'Who is there?' asked Albert once again. 'The Queen of England!' declared the Queen. Yet a third time came the question 'Who is there?' And a voice answered softly, 'Your wife, Albert.'

The door swung open. After every outburst, the Queen was full of remorse and resolved to be more worthy of her angel. After all, Albert, she believed, was a superior being and it was she who had to improve herself.

With his love of order and efficiency, Albert set about reorganising the royal household, which was in chaos, with far too many servants and far too much waste. One department laid the fires, while another lit them, which meant the fires were frequently not lit at all. One department cleaned the outside of the windows, another the inside, which meant the windows were usually dirty. At Buckingham Palace the drains smelled terribly, meals were always late and guests got hopelessly lost and wandered the corridors for hours (one barged into what he hoped was his own room and found Her Majesty having her hair brushed). Albert's new system made him unpopular but saved the Queen a good deal of money. And in the end, Victoria gave in over Lehzen too – her old governess was given a pension and sent back to Germany.

CHAPTER SIX

However much the Queen dreaded pregnancy and ugly babies, she kept on having them. After Vicky and Bertie, came Alice, born in 1843, Alfred, in 1844, Helena in 1846, Louise in 1848, Arthur in 1850, Leopold in 1853, and ninth, and last, Beatrice in 1857. Amazingly, at a time when so many children died young, all the princes and princesses were strong and healthy. All, that is, except Leopold who was born with haemophilia (a condition which prevents the blood from clotting). Like a delicate piece of china, he had to be handled with care.

Photographs of Victoria and Albert and the children appeared – it was the first time ordinary people had been able to see what their royal family looked like, in fact it was the first time there had ever been such a royal family, free of scandal and skeletons. Here was a model of what a family should be; a shining example to the British people.

Victoria and Albert were fond, but strict parents. Bertie, the Prince of Wales, was a particular worry. Beside Vicky, Albert's favourite, who was quick and clever, Bertie seemed slow and backward. Even Alice, his younger sister, was ahead of him at lessons. And he had such tantrums; he was so disobedient and rude. As Britain's future King, it was most important, believed Victoria and Albert, that Bertie should be properly instructed and made aware of his duty. Mr Birch, his tutor, of whom Bertie was very fond, was dismissed for being too lenient. With his new tutor, the hapless Bertie was shut away with his books seven hours a day, six days a week and never allowed to mix with other boys.

Still, it wasn't all work. The royal children were taken to the latest attractions – Madame Tussaud's and the zoo in Regent's Park. And 'General' (not a real General) Tom Thumb, the 37-inch American dwarf, performed three times for the royal family. Tom Thumb had been appearing in Barnum's 'Greatest Show on

Earth'. When the royal summons came, Phineas T. Barnum fixed a notice to the theatre door – 'Closed this evening, General Tom Thumb being at Buckingham Palace by command of Her Majesty'. At the palace, the General shook hands with the Queen, sang and danced, did his repertoire of imitations and chatted to Albert. As he backed out of the room, the Queen's poodle became overexcited and started yapping and snapping at his heels. Her Majesty sent a message – she hoped no damage had been done.

As the children multiplied, Victoria and Albert began to long for a home other than Windsor or Buckingham Palace, for somewhere more private away from London. In 1843 they bought Osborne House on the Isle of Wight. The old house was pulled down and a spanking new one built to Albert's design – comfortable, not too big, a family house. It had every mod-con – gas-lighting, baths (and showers too) with hot and cold running water, and water closets (lavatories), which were extremely rare in 1843.

For the children there was a very grand kind of Wendy House, built to look like a Swiss cottage. Here they displayed their natural history collections, or played with a miniature shop called 'Spratt's Grocer to Her Majesty', which had tiny sacks and jars and bottles full of real food and drink. The cottage had a proper kitchen, with a child-sized cooking range and utensils, where the girls learned to bake cakes. Outside they tended their garden plots (each child had a wheelbarrow and garden tools marked with his or her initials) or played in the Victoria fort, which was a model fort, with a drawbridge and cannon, that the princes had helped build for the Queen's birthday.

Victoria liked to celebrate her birthdays at Osborne. The day would begin with a band playing on the terrace below her room. The children would gather at the bottom of the stairs, holding nosegays, waiting to greet their mother and lead her to the 'Present Room', where a birthday table stood decorated with flowers and heaped with gifts. In the evening there would be dancing.

Osborne was a place for family life and there the Queen spent some of her happiest times. She delighted in watching Albert dragging the children around the nursery in a basket, or helping them catch butterflies, or playing hide and seek, or turning somersaults in the hay to make them laugh. Secretly, though, she longed to have her husband all to herself.

At Osborne, in July 1847, the Queen announced she wished to take a dip in the sea. Elaborate preparations were made as the royal modesty had to be preserved at all costs. A bathing machine – like a changing hut on wheels – was pulled, by a horse, to the water's edge. The Queen entered through a door at the back, was helped by a dresser into a voluminous bathing costume and a floppy hat and came out at the front on to a platform from which, hidden by curtains, she walked down some steps into the sea. Once she was submerged the machine was removed.

'I thought it delightful till I put my head under the water, when I thought I should be stifled,' she wrote. After she had splashed and wallowed around for a while, like a small hippopotamus, an attendant rang a bell, the machine was brought back and the Queen disappeared from view.

As well as Osborne, Victoria and Albert decided they needed a Scottish retreat. They both felt at home in Scotland. The Highland landscape reminded Albert of the forests and lakes of Germany and Victoria was a great believer in the benefits of bracing Scottish air. They bought the estate of Balmoral and once again Albert designed a house. It was all as Scottish as could be – tartan everywhere you looked, Albert and the princes wearing kilts, porridge for breakfast, reels after dinner. When in residence, the Queen even seemed to speak with a faint Scottish accent.

Guests and ministers dreaded visits to Balmoral, as the house was so uncomfortable and so unbearably cold (worse than Siberia, said the Tsar of Russia). The Queen kept thermometers in every room and the minute the temperature rose to a level that she considered unhealthy, the windows were thrown open. She, however, was blissfully happy. She would sketch and make surprise visits to Highlanders in their crofts (the Queen was particularly fond of the Highland people and there were few things she liked better than sitting down for a chat and a snack of boiled potatoes). Albert would go shooting, and the whole family would take ponies and picnics and set off on long expeditions into the hills.

CHAPTER SEVEN

1848, the Year of Revolutions – when Victoria sat a little less comfortably on her throne; when the French King, Louis Philippe, was toppled from his; when the call to revolution was heard all over Europe.

In Britain, the Industrial Revolution was spreading its great machines, its factories and foundries, its smoke and grime across the country. The hum of change was in the air – a whirring and a grinding and a roaring. And a ringing of tills. For Britain was becoming rich. The steel and iron and textile industries were booming. Canals and railways were being built. The new steamships chugged British goods around the world.

But, as the rich grew richer, the poor grew poorer. The factory owner could twirl his watch chain and dine off the finest china, but the factory worker was lucky not to die of cholera from drinking putrid water, and luckier still if he could buy bread for his children. And those children were put to work themselves. In the cotton mills small boys ducked under vast, clanking machines to scavenge cotton fluff. In match factories young girls were poisoned by noxious fumes.

People were beginning to protest at such inequality and injustice. A group known as the Chartists called for reform. They wanted every man, not just those who owned property or land, to have the right to vote, which would mean that the poor at least had a say in how they were governed. On April 10th 1848 the Chartists set off to present parliament with a petition. It had been signed by two million people and it filled two hackney cabs.

There were rumours that 150,000 people would march through the streets of London and the old Duke of Wellington was called out to defend the city. The Queen was seriously alarmed – could this be the beginning of revolution? Would she find herself fleeing her country like Louis Philippe? To be on the safe side, the royal family did flee, to Osborne. In fact the demonstration passed off perfectly peacefully – there were only about 20,000 people and it poured with rain.

The trouble was that, surrounded by her family, protected by her ministers, far away at Osborne or Balmoral, there was much that the Queen simply didn't see. She didn't see the poor in the workhouses, the five-year-old children working ten hours a day in the mines, or the thousands dying of starvation in Ireland because the potato crop had failed. When she was made aware of the suffering of her subjects, she was full of compassion and determination that something must be done. But, as for Chartists, or Republicans (who wanted to get rid of the monarchy), she had no time for them. 'I maintain that revolutions are always bad for the country,' she said.

No Victorian, rich or poor, could ignore the way the world was changing. By 1850 you could have gaslight in your home, you could buy a penny postage stamp and send a letter, you could take a photograph and travel on a train. Victoria and Albert's first train journey was from Windsor to Paddington, in 1842. It took 23 minutes, at 44 miles per hour – too fast for Albert's liking – 'Not so fast, Mr Conductor, next time if you please,' he admonished. Still, Albert was the first to admit that PROGRESS was the order of the day and what better way to celebrate progress, he thought, than to hold a Great Exhibition.

The Great Exhibition was intended to be a showcase for manufacturing and design from all over the world. It opened on May 1st 1851. The Queen drove up to what looked like a gigantic greenhouse in Hyde Park. This was Crystal Palace, built by Joseph Paxton from 300,000 panes of glass. Its domed roof rose right over Hyde Park's great elm trees. The Queen, sparkling almost as much as the building, wore a pink and silver dress, a diamond as big as an egg, and a crown. When she walked through the doors and saw the cheering crowds, a fountain sending up cascades of water, row upon row of exhibits, everything brilliant with light and colour, she felt quite overcome with pride and delight in Albert's achievement – 'It was the *happiest, proudest* day of my life,' she wrote.

With Bertie and Vicky she wandered, entranced, marvelling at Indian silks, Persian carpets, German porcelain, a medal-making machine, Chubb locks, a knife with 300 blades, an alarm bed that ejected the sleeper, a garden seat made of coal. Six million people visited the exhibition and the profits were used to build the museums that stand today in South Kensington.

In 1854, with the Great Exhibition a glorious but fading memory, the Queen found herself facing the first war of her reign: the Crimean War. Russia had been attacking lands in Eastern Europe that belonged to Turkey. The Russians, it was felt, simply could not be allowed to continue expanding eastwards. They had to be taught a lesson. So Britain and France joined the Turks and declared war on Russia. The Queen took a keen interest in proceedings and proudly waved off the troops.

But news from the Crimea – in Southern Russia – was grim. For all their bravery, British soldiers were being slaughtered in disastrous battles such as the battle of Balaclava, where the cavalry were mown down as they charged what turned out to be the wrong guns (this was the Charge of the Light Brigade). If they didn't succumb to bayonets or bullets, the troops froze to death in blizzards, or died of cholera, dysentery and malaria. There wasn't enough food; supplies weren't getting through; the generals made one blunder after another. The dreadful conditions in the hospitals, where bodies were piled high in corridors swimming with sewage, were at least improved by a nurse called Florence Nightingale.

The Queen, however, grew more and more distressed by the reports of the suffering of her troops. She longed to be a man so that she could fight alongside them. Failing that, she busied herself knitting socks and scarves and presenting medals to returning soldiers, many of whom were horribly mutilated. She was moved to see how thrilled they were to touch her hand – 'the rough hand of the brave and honest private soldier came for the first time in contact with that of their Sovereign and their Queen! Noble fellows! I own I feel as if they were my own children,' she wrote.

Who was to blame for this war where men died so pointlessly? The generals? The government? The Prime Minister, Lord Aberdeen, felt responsible and resigned. He was replaced by Lord Palmerston. When Palmerston had been Foreign Secretary a few years before, the Queen had greatly disliked him – he had seemed to do just as he pleased, without ever consulting her. The country, she'd felt, wasn't safe in his hands. Now Palmerston was a deaf old man with false teeth that tended to fall out. But his wits were still sharp and the Queen accepted that he was the man for the job.

CHAPTER EIGHT

Since France, not so long ago England's great enemy, was now her ally against Russia, it was decided that the French Emperor, Louis Napoleon III, and the Empress Eugenie should be invited to England. The Queen did not expect to think much of the Emperor – he had, after all, deposed a king. And he certainly wasn't much to look at, with his huge head perched on a stunted body and a tuft of black hair sprouting from beneath his bottom lip. But he flattered Victoria outrageously and she found herself charmed and fascinated.

'*Comme tu es belle*!' he murmured softly into her ear at a ball, as he whirled her into a waltz. And she twinkled back up at him. The Emperor seemed thrillingly mysterious and 'very extraordinary'. She was charmed by the beautiful Empress too.

It was Empress Eugenie who brought the first crinoline to England. The crinoline was a dress worn over a petticoat that had steel hoops sewn into it to make it stiff. This created an enormously wide skirt, sometimes as much as six feet across. It also made sitting down and passing through narrow doorways a tricky business. But crinolines were soon all the rage – 'crinolinomania' it was called – worn by everyone from queens to scullery maids. On the tall, graceful Empress, the crinoline looked wonderfully elegant. It did nothing for the Queen, who, after years of guzzling chocolate cake and trifle, was already as round and wide as a barrel. It was lucky that she didn't the least bit care how she looked.

Such a success was the Emperor's visit that a few months later Victoria and Albert, with Bertie and Vicky, sailed to France in the royal yacht. They were driven around Paris; they went to Versailles; there were dinners and balls and fireworks. The French couldn't get over how dowdy Victoria was, with her huge bonnets stuck with streamers and feathers and her hideous handbags. But, dowdy or not, they recognised that here was a true queen. She did not seem to walk so much as glide, as though invisible wheels were attached to her boots. And at the opera, after bowing graciously to the crowds, she would sit down *without* checking to make sure her chair was still in place. Queens, believed Victoria, never need look behind them.

With Palmerston in charge, reports from the Crimea were more encouraging and in September 1855 Sebastopol, the great Russian fort, fell. The war was over. The Queen was at Balmoral when she heard the news and she watched as cheering servants, gentlemen and ladies of the household and villagers streamed up the hill to light a huge bonfire, dance and drink whisky.

Not long after the fall of Sebastopol, Prince Frederick William of Prussia, known as Fritz, arrived at Balmoral. For some time Victoria and Albert had looked on 24-year-old Fritz as a possible husband for Vicky, though she was still only 14. Not only would Fritz one day be King of Prussia and Emperor of Germany, he was also tall, handsome and kind-hearted. On his first morning, Fritz came to find Albert in the library. 'Sir, might I be allowed the honour of joining your family?' asked Fritz hesitantly. Albert gave a brief nod – 'Ve vould velcome you,' he said. Encouraged, Fritz continued, 'May I then ask the Princess Royal for her hand?' Permission was granted.

Fritz seized his chance while he and Vicky were out riding. He began to talk to her about Germany and then asked – 'Could you ever consider living in Prussia?'

'I think that perhaps I could,' replied Vicky in a very small voice.

Fritz bent down, picked a sprig of white heather and held it out to her as he said – 'I have loved you from the moment I first saw you. You would make me the happiest man in the world if you would consent to be my wife.'

Vicky blushed deeply – 'I too would be happy,' she mumbled, 'but I must speak to my parents.' And they shook hands.

Back at Balmoral, trembling with suppressed excitement, she hurried to Victoria and Albert. 'Have you anything to tell us?' asked her father.

'Oh yes! A great deal! It is that the Prince has asked me to marry him,' she replied in a rush.

'And do you feel the same about Fritz as he does about you?' put in her mother.

'Oh, I have always loved him!' said Vicky, her eyes shining, as Fritz came into the room and she threw herself into his arms.

She's still a child, thought the Queen, but she's marrying for love, as I did. The engagement was announced, although the wedding had to wait until Vicky was 17. In the meantime her mother insisted on chaperoning the couple – they could only be alone together if she was in the next door room with the door left OPEN.

The Queen was most indignant when word came from Prussia that the wedding should be held in Berlin. She instantly dismissed such a ridiculous idea – 'The assumption of its being *too much* for a Prince Royal of Prussia to come over to marry the Princess Royal of Great Britain IN England is too absurd… it is not *every* day that one marries the eldest daughter of the Queen of England,' she wrote.

When the wedding eventually took place, in London, in January 1858, Victoria felt as if she was getting married herself, only more nervous, and when she and Albert said their goodbyes to their daughter, as snow fell steadily around them, everyone was in tears. Afterwards Albert wrote to Vicky, his favourite child, 'I am not of a demonstrative nature and therefore you can hardly know how dear you have always been to me and what a void you have left behind in my heart.' The Queen wrote to her daughter two or three times a week for the rest of her life.

CHAPTER NINE

Britain was not just becoming a rich nation, it also boasted a GREAT and GLORIOUS Empire, of which most Victorians, and above all the Queen, were enormously proud. You only had to look at a map to see how much of the world – India, Canada, Australia, New Zealand, parts of Africa and the West Indies – was coloured pink, showing that these were colonies, governed by Britain. But the colonies weren't always so happy to be governed – after all, what right did Britain have to help herself to other people's countries?

The administration of India was in the hands of the East India company, which had originally been a trading company but now represented the British government. Some felt the company wasn't doing a very good job. In 1857, amid a general feeling of unrest, a rumour began that gun carriages, given to native soldiers, had been greased with pig and cow fat, which was deeply offensive to both Muslims and Hindus. Three Indian regiments rose up against their white superiors. The mutiny spread through the north of India and there were tales of dreadful atrocities committed by Indians. At the garrison of Cawnpore the bodies of British women and children, butchered in cold blood, were thrown down a well, where their tangled, naked limbs glowed palely in the gloom. Of course, the British took bloody revenge and the bodies of mutineers (sometimes alive) were fired from the mouths of canon.

The Queen was appalled by such violence. She was fascinated by India – the 'jewel in her crown' she said – and she liked and respected Indians. She realised that brutally punishing the rebels would only make things worse – 'They should know that there is no hatred to a brown skin – none, but the greatest wish on the Queen's part to see them happy, contented and flourishing,' she said. She firmly believed in respecting the religious beliefs and customs of other races. Plans were made to abolish the East India Company and to put India under the direct rule of the Queen and her government. Victoria couldn't hide her glee – '*All*... to be mine,' she wrote.

The Queen was satisfied too when, in 1857, it was agreed that she could give Albert an English royal title (she'd have made him King if she could). No longer was he merely a German prince. Now he was Prince Consort. But his new title didn't seem to greatly cheer up Albert himself. These days he was a picture of gloom. He was not yet 40, but looked much older. The slim figure, the soft waves of hair, the delicate complexion, were long gone. He was paunchy, pale, balding and constantly ailing with one thing or another (he felt the cold so in the early mornings that he took to wearing a wig).

Duty sat heavily on the Prince Consort's shoulders. It was work, work, work, from dawn till dusk. Every morning he would sit at his desk, light the green lamp he had brought with him from Germany and methodically start on his mountain of papers (by now Albert had taken over much of Victoria's work). If the Queen tried to talk to him he'd snap, '*Store mich nicht, ich lese das fertig*' ('Don't disturb me, I am busy reading').

Sometimes she felt quite hurt.

Albert greatly missed his daughter Vicky. In the autumn of 1860 he and Victoria went to Germany to visit her and see their first grandson, Prince William of Prussia. While Victoria and Vicky were sketching one day, Albert had a carriage accident. He wasn't seriously hurt, but he seemed very shaken. 'His nervous system is easily excited and he's so completely overpowered by everything,' Victoria wrote. A few days later he went for a walk with his brother Ernest and, as they stood looking out at the hills of Gotha, tears suddenly started rolling down Albert's cheeks. 'This is the last time I shall stand here,' he said.

But by Christmas Albert seemed less careworn. The royal family, apart from Vicky, were at Windsor. It was under Victoria and Albert that Christmas came to be celebrated much as it is today. People began to send Christmas cards and decorate trees and pull crackers. It was Albert in fact who brought the Christmas tree, which was a German custom, to England.

That year at Windsor there were several small trees hung with candles, toffees and paper chains, with presents piled beneath them. Ten-year-old Prince

Arthur unwrapped a toy rifle and took a pot-shot at his father. Everyone tucked into turkey, goose, beef and plum pudding. Albert swung baby Beatrice in a dinner napkin. Precocious Beatrice, the Queen's ninth and last child, made everyone laugh. 'Baby mustn't have that, it's not good for Baby,' said her mother one day at lunch. 'But she likes it, my dear,' replied Baby, helping herself. After a sharp frost, the lake froze solid and Albert put on his skates (he was an expert skater) and glided and twirled as his wife looked on admiringly. Little did she know it was to be her last truly happy Christmas.

In March 1861 the Queen's mother, the Duchess of Kent, lay dying at Frogmore, her Windsor house. Victoria's old resentment towards her mother, for always siding with Sir John Conroy, had long vanished. For her part, the Duchess admitted that she had been foolish to put so much trust in Conroy. Encouraged by Albert, mother and daughter had grown closer over the years. Now the Queen sat at her mother's bedside and held her hand as she drew her last breaths. 'The dreaded terrible calamity has befallen us, which seems like an awful dream... Oh God! How awful! How mysterious!… the constant crying was a comfort and relief… but oh! The agony of it!' she wrote.

Victoria's reaction to death had always been extreme: the deaths of Albert's father, a man she barely knew, and of the old Duke of Wellington had brought on absolute floods of tears. At the loss of her mother she became quite hysterical. Going through the Duchess's papers she realised how much her mother had really loved her and was stricken by remorse for the times she'd treated her coldly. For three weeks she ate all her meals alone. Some feared she might go mad with grief. Indeed there were rumours that she *had* gone mad and been confined to a padded cell. Albert tried to cheer her by taking her to Osborne.

But Albert himself was far from well. 'I do not cling to life,' he once told his wife, 'You do, but I set no store by it… I am sure if I had a severe illness I should give up at once.'

Every part of his body pained him. Yet still, every morning, he dragged himself out of bed, lit the green lamp and took up his pen. Thanks to Albert, Britain avoided being drawn into a war with America (where civil war was raging). It was the last act of Albert the

Good for the country that had come to appreciate him.

His son, the Prince of Wales, only added to his worries. Bertie had continued to disappoint his parents. They didn't see that he was actually a perfectly intelligent, affectionate and sweet-natured boy. Albert thought him a hopeless lazybones, far too fond of fine clothes and even fonder of eating, drinking and going to the races. Bertie was supposed to be improving himself for the good of the country he would one day rule, not having fun. Victoria couldn't resist dwelling on Bertie's looks – his head was so small, his features so large, and then there was the 'total want of chin' (for which he had her to thank of course). If only, she sighed, he could have been more like his father.

Now that he was 20 it was necessary for Bertie to marry. His parents had even found him a suitable bride – the beautiful Princess Alexandra of Denmark. But Bertie seemed strangely reluctant. His lack of enthusiasm was explained when, in the autumn of 1861, rumours came to Albert's ears that Bertie was infatuated with a pretty actress. Albert was mortified. He decided to go to Cambridge, where Bertie was studying, to confront his son. As they paced the damp streets, Albert reproached Bertie for having 'sunk into vice and debauchery' and Bertie hung his head in shame. The chill seeped into Albert's aching bones and he returned to Windsor feeling worse than ever.

There were signs that Albert might have typhoid, but the royal doctors kept insisting that there was no cause for alarm and the Queen clung to their words. Albert's nights were sleepless. During the day he insisted on getting up, half delirious, and restlessly moving from room to room. Victoria followed him, wringing her hands.

When, at last, the doctors announced that it *was* typhoid, Albert was confined to bed in the Blue Room and nursed by his daughter Princess Alice (the Queen was too distraught to be much help). He asked Alice if she had told Vicky about his illness.

'Yes,' she replied, 'I told her you were very ill.'

'You did wrong,' whispered Albert, 'You should have told her I was dying. Yes, I am dying.'

On December 8th, when the Queen came to his bedside, he didn't recognise her – '*Wer is das?*' (who is that) he asked.

'*Weibchen*' (your little wife) replied the Queen, weeping.

'*Das ist recht. Gutes Weibchen*' (That's right. Good little wife), said Albert, patting her hand.

On December 13th Alice summoned the Prince of Wales, who hurried up from Cambridge, and the next day, as the end drew near, the children came in to kiss their father's hand. Then it was the turn of the Queen to lean over and ask for '*ein Kuss*'. A last kiss. Struggling to control her tears, she left the room for a moment, but as she did so a dry rasping came from Albert's throat.

'It's the death rattle!' cried Alice, and called her mother back in. The Queen rushed to the bed. Too late. She fell upon the lifeless body and a terrible wail rang through the palace – 'Oh my dear darling!'

Later, as Victoria lay on a sofa, with her children and members of the royal household hovering helplessly around her, she held out a plump white hand and said imploringly, 'You will not desert me? You will all help me?'

That night the bell of St Paul's tolled mournfully, in memory of Albert the Good. And there were many who asked themselves the question – how would the Queen carry on?

CHAPTER TEN

'My life as a happy one is ended! The world is gone for me!' wrote the 'utterly broken-hearted and crushed widow of 42', to her uncle Leopold. What point was there in living herself, except for the sakes of her children and her country? How could she contemplate life without Albert? He who had been everything to her. She hadn't done so much as choose a bonnet without his advice.

Every night the Queen went to bed clutching Albert's nightshirt. She gave orders that the Blue Room, where he had died, should be left exactly as it was. Every evening Albert's dressing-gown and clean clothes were placed on his bed and a jug of hot water put on his washstand. The glass, from which he had taken his last sip of medicine, was kept on the table beside the bed. It stayed there for 40 years. His blotting paper and pen lay on the writing table. It was as if at any minute Albert himself might wander in and sit down. Albert the angel became a saint.

The Queen wore black for the rest of her life. Her handkerchiefs and writing paper were edged with deep black borders. Indeed the whole country was plunged into mourning, and mourning in Victorian England was a serious business. Stores sold out of black cloth. Away went the brilliantly coloured crinolines, the flounces and lace, the diamonds and pearls. Out came the plainest of dresses in dusty black crêpe and bombazine, mourning jewellery made of jet, even black underwear.

There was an added bitterness to Victoria's grief. Quite unjustly, she insisted that Bertie was responsible for Albert's death, that the scandal of Bertie's romance with the actress had killed his father. She could hardly bear to look at her son and, when, in 1862, he left the country for a tour of Europe, she felt quite relieved to see the back of him. But by the time he returned, the Queen had had a change of heart. She accepted that Bertie was blameless and she was extremely pleased to hear that he was to marry Princess Alexandra. The Queen thoroughly approved of 'Alix'. It was only to be hoped that she would be a good influence on Bertie.

The young couple were married in May 1863, in the chapel at Windsor. The Queen, wearing widow's weeds, naturally, sat apart from the congregation, in the Royal Closet above the altar. Amongst the congregation was an up-and-coming politician called Benjamin Disraeli, who received an icy glare for daring to peer at Her Majesty through his monocle. Also present was the Queen's grandson, Prince William of Prussia (the future German Kaiser, who, as Kaiser Bill, would become Britain's enemy in World War I). At four years old he was already causing trouble. That morning he had ruffled royal feathers by calling his grandmother 'Duck' and now he sank his teeth, hard, into the legs of his uncles Alfred and Leopold. A wedding lunch followed the service. The Queen did not attend.

As for performing public duties, well, that was out of the question. The burden of ruling a country was just too much to bear alone. For meetings with the Privy Council the Queen sat in one room and the Councillors in another, while they shouted to each other through an open door. She couldn't possibly open parliament. 'Whatever the poor Queen can do she will, but she will not be dictated to,' she wrote to the Prime Minister, Lord Russell (the Queen was always 'the Queen' in letters to her ministers, never an 'I'). She shut herself away at Osborne or Balmoral.

Her children, her secretaries, her ministers, tiptoed around her. What if she did go mad, like her grandfather George III? Sometimes she would tap her forehead with her stubby fingers muttering – 'My reason! My reason!' No one wanted to force the Queen to do her duty. Yet rumbles of discontent could be heard. Someone tied a notice to the rails of Buckingham Palace – 'These commanding premises to be let or sold, in consequence of the late occupant's declining business'. Victoria hadn't appeared in public for nearly two years. What was the use of a sovereign who never showed her face?

The Queen had built her grief around her like a fortress and she might well have locked herself away within its walls for ever. That she didn't was thanks to two very different men. One was a rough-and-ready

Scottish servant and the other was a silver-tongued Tory politician.

CHAPTER ELEVEN

During the winter of 1864 Victoria began riding again, and a gillie, who had accompanied Albert when he went shooting, came from Balmoral to lead her pony. His name was John Brown and, Victoria wrote, he was 'a real comfort, for he is so devoted to me – so simple, so intelligent, so unlike an ordinary servant'. Brown was tall and strapping, with blue eyes and a firm jaw.

Soon the Queen couldn't do without him. He was given the grand title of 'The Queen's Highland Servant', his salary was increased and he had privileges allowed to no one else. Brown did much more than heave Her Majesty onto her pony – he became her personal protector. He accompanied her on her travels to Europe, where his kilt and bare knees caused a stir.

Brown loathed travelling, but Victoria much enjoyed setting off on her royal train, with her servants, cooks and doctors – as many as 100 people – her horses and ponies, her donkey, her carriages. Even her bed came with her.

The Queen could strike terror into the stoutest of hearts and she ruled over her family and Household with a rod of iron. The strictest etiquette was observed at all times. Only when the Queen herself left the palace could anyone else go outside. And then they were expected to keep out of sight. If word came that Her Majesty was approaching, grown men and women would scatter and run for the nearest tree with cries of 'The Queen! The Queen!'

Because she violently disapproved of smoking, gentlemen would resort to lying on the floor of their bedrooms holding their cigarettes up the chimney. A maid of honour once complained that she had rheumatism in her legs and Victoria replied coldly, 'When I became sovereign, ladies didn't have legs.' And woe betide a maid of honour who wanted to get married – that went down very badly. If the Queen no longer had the happiness of a husband, why should anyone else?

But the Queen held no terror for Brown. Once, helping her to tie her bonnet, he remarked 'Hoots then wumman! Can ye no hold yerr head up?' When he didn't approve of a dress she was wearing, he'd scowl and say, 'What's this ye've got on today?' Once Victoria told him, 'You make the best cup of tea I've ever tasted.' Brown, who liked a tipple, replied, 'Well it should be Ma'am. I put a grand nip o'whisky in it.'

The Queen was always considerate towards her servants, but Brown wasn't just a servant. He was a friend; he made her laugh; he wasn't afraid to speak his mind or to contradict her. And she liked him for it. She greatly appreciated his devotion and returned it with her own. Out riding one day she told him, 'No one loves you more than I do, Brown. You have no better friend than me.'

'Nor you than me. No one loves you more,' came the reply. With Brown at her side she felt safe, and public duties were less daunting. She even agreed to open parliament in 1866, though she said it felt like going to an execution.

But Brown was very unpopular among the royal household and the Queen's children. They thought he had far too much influence. They objected to the way he would barge into rooms without knocking. He was rude and too big for his boots and was often to be found lying in a drunken stupor on his bed. He was surely not a fit person to have Her Majesty's ear. The gossip started – some called the Queen 'Mrs Brown' and said that she had secretly married her servant. There were even rumours that she had given birth to his baby. But the Queen was oblivious. She wouldn't hear a word against him; she turned a blind eye to his drunkenness. Of course, nobody could ever replace beloved Albert, but Brown was a great comfort and surely she was allowed that.

As for the second man who tempted the Queen out of seclusion, he was none other than the politician who had once so impertinently examined her through his monocle: Benjamin Disraeli. When Disraeli became Prime Minister in February 1868, he received a royal summons to Osborne. The Queen waited for him in the Council Room, where she always saw her ministers. The French windows, through which the English Channel glittered in the distance, were ajar, as usual, and the room was icy cold.

Disraeli, shivering noticeably, came through the door – a funny-looking creature, she thought, with his dyed black ringlets and goatee beard, his dead-white skin and flashing sloe eyes. And then he was on his knees in front of her, kissing her hands and saying, 'I plight my troth to the kindest of Mistresses!' Suddenly, the Queen's glum expression was transformed by the sunniest of smiles – 'Perhaps you would care to sit down, Mr Disraeli,' she said, waving a hand towards a chair (she hadn't asked a Prime Minister to sit down in her presence since Lord Melbourne). It was a happy beginning.

Like Brown, Disraeli understood how to manage the Queen. Behind her back he called her 'the Faery', and his secret was to treat her like a woman – to profess undying devotion, to talk to her like a poet not a politician, to even flirt a little. Disraeli wrote novels and Victoria was very proud of a book *she* had published about her life in Scotland, which became a bestseller (her children, however, thought it highly embarrassing; 'twaddle' said the Prince of Wales). When Disraeli put his head on one side, smiled winningly and murmured, 'We authors, Ma'am,' she glowed with pleasure.

'Everyone likes flattery and when it comes to royalty, you should lay it on with a trowel,' he said. And it worked wonders with the Queen.

She greatly looked forward to her meetings with her Prime Minister and his long, gossipy letters. 'He is full of poetry, romance and chivalry,' she said. She regularly sent him primroses from Osborne. She even sent him a Valentine's card. He made her feel quite skittish and, more importantly, he made her take an interest in the business of being a queen again.

But she was still most reluctant to appear in public. Her 'shattered nerves and health', she claimed, would not allow it. Some thought that these were just excuses and that she was clinging to her misery (the Queen, said one of her secretaries, is 'roaring well and can do everything she likes and nothing she doesn't'). Her children got together and wrote a letter warning her that she was putting the monarchy in real danger by hiding away. Why, people started asking, should they pay for a queen they hardly ever saw? And why, when there was a war – France was now fighting Prussia – did she always take the side of the Germans? The Republicans were a group who wanted to get rid of the monarchy altogether. Their voices became louder and louder. Who needed a queen anyway?

In the summer of 1871, at Balmoral, Victoria became ill and there was no doubting it was genuine. She had a very painful abscess on her arm, she couldn't walk and she lost two stone in weight. By the autumn she had more or less recovered, but in November Bertie was diagnosed with typhoid, the disease that had probably killed his father.

Victoria still disapproved of Bertie, for his unsuitable friends and his love of gambling, smoking and pretty women, but she admitted that he was a good, affectionate son. She flew to his bedside, at Sandringham, Bertie's Norfolk estate, and found him delirious and raving (he imagined himself to be king). On December 13th the disease reached its crisis, and it looked as if Bertie might actually die on the very anniversary of Albert's death. The dreaded 14th dawned and, a miracle! The crisis passed. Bertie opened his eyes and said, 'Oh! Dear Mama, I am so glad to see you. Have you been here all this time?'

The Queen agreed that the recovery of the heir to the throne called for a public Thanksgiving Service. She and Bertie rode together to St Paul's in an open carriage. She lifted Bertie's hand and kissed it as the crowds cheered and roared their heads off. It was a 'wonderful demonstration of loyalty and affection from the very highest to the lowest', wrote the Queen. Londoners danced in the streets long into the night. No one was listening to the Republicans any more; suddenly the Queen had never been so popular.

She became even more so when, two days later, while she was out in her carriage, she felt the cold brush of metal against the side of her head. It was a youth with a pistol. 'Save me!' she cried.

Instantly, John Brown's strong arm seized the boy by the throat. He was Arthur O'Connor, aged 17, his pistol was unloaded and he was clearly insane. Even so, everyone agreed it was monstrous that their Queen should be attacked in this way (and for the sixth time). The Queen thought it was almost worth being shot at 'to see how much she was loved'. She asked for Arthur to be transported and he happily agreed, so long, he said, as it was somewhere with plenty of sunshine.

CHAPTER TWELVE

By 1873, the blackest days of the Queen's grief were over, though Albert, of course, was never for a minute forgotten. On a visit to Florence she even stood in front of the cathedral and held up a miniature portrait of her husband, so he could enjoy it too. But the Queen couldn't help feeling that Albert had somehow given up (he died for 'want of pluck' she once said). There was to be no giving up for Victoria. She was only 55 and she was a queen. In fact she felt she deserved to be more than a queen – she wanted to be an empress.

The King of Prussia called himself Emperor, so did the Tsar of Russia. Why couldn't she? India belonged to the British crown – how about Empress of India? She certainly felt like an empress – 'I am an Empress and in common conversation am sometimes called Empress of India' – this was nonsense – 'Why have I never officially assumed this title?' she asked. Surely Disraeli could make it possible. And Disraeli did, even though quite a lot of M.P.s objected. On May 12th 1876 Victoria became Empress of India. At a dinner to celebrate her new title, she sailed into the room, bristling with jewels given to her by Indian maharajahs.

She didn't just begin to interest herself in politics and public affairs again, she tried to use her influence. When, in April 1877, Russia declared war on Turkey, the Queen was outraged – those beastly Russians were trying to dominate the East and must be stopped and if that meant British soldiers should fight, so be it. She told Disraeli as much. 'Oh, if the Queen were a man she would like to go and give the Russians such a beating,' she cried. In fact Britain did not join the war and Disraeli helped bring about peace between Russia and Turkey. But the Queen felt quite invigorated by the excitement. She gave a dance and waltzed for the first time in 18 years.

Victoria didn't believe in war for war's sake, but she firmly believed that Britain must never become a 'laughing stock' abroad. 'If we are to maintain our position as a first-rate Power,' she wrote to Disraeli, 'we must, with our Indian Empire and large Colonies, be prepared for attacks and wars, somewhere or other CONTINUALLY.'

In 1880 the Tories lost the election and the Liberals (as the old Whig party had become) were returned to power. For the Queen, this meant accepting the Liberal leader, William Gladstone, as her prime minister. It was a horrible prospect – she had greatly disliked Gladstone when he had been prime minister six years before – and she did all she could to prevent it. As queen, Victoria was not meant to favour either party, but she couldn't help herself when it came to prime ministers.

'The great alarm in the country is Mr Gladstone,' she wrote to her Private Secretary, 'and the Queen will sooner abdicate than send for or have any communication with that half-mad firebrand who will soon ruin everything and be a Dictator.' There was, however, no alternative and the 'half-mad firebrand' it was.

Gladstone was a very different kettle of fish to Disraeli and the Queen loathed the one as much as she loved the other. The fact that Gladstone was enormously popular with the public – the 'people's William' they called him – didn't help matters. It wasn't so much his politics as that he didn't know how to treat her. Disraeli had told her everything, but Gladstone, complained Victoria, kept her 'completely in the dark'. And when he did consult her he was so dreadfully earnest. 'The Queen won't stand dictation. She won't be a machine,' declared Victoria. Yet that's exactly what Gladstone did – he dictated. He talked to her, she said, as if she was a 'public meeting'.

Gladstone and the Liberals believed in reform, in improving the lot of the poor. They brought in new laws to allow more men to vote (votes for women, which the Queen thought a very bad idea, were still a long way off); to provide education for the children of the poor; to get rid of the worst slums. The Queen felt particularly strongly about better housing. There were huge numbers of homeless in British cities by the 1880s and people had taken to sleeping in open coffins. The Queen was told of a family of seven who had to share one bed. 'I should have slept on the floor,' she remarked. But she approved of Gladstone's efforts to improve such conditions.

She *didn't* approve of his policy towards Ireland. Ireland was a significant problem during Victoria's reign and one the Queen never understood. Ireland had been under British rule since the 17th century and wretched had been the lives of many ordinary Irishmen and women as a result. In 1846 the failure of the potato crop brought terrible famine. A million people died. During the hungry years that followed another million emigrated, in desperation, to America. A group called the Fenians believed the Irish should be allowed to rule themselves (this was called Home Rule) and to bring this about they were prepared to resort to violence. They planted bombs and plotted attacks on the Queen.

While Gladstone passionately supported Home Rule, Victoria just as passionately opposed it. She thought Gladstone was far too soft on the Irish. She was appalled when two young Englishmen – the new Irish Secretary and his Under Secretary – were knifed to death in Dublin. It proved, she thought, just how mistaken Gladstone's policy was. 'The state of Ireland causes the Queen much painful thought and must she thinks do so to Mr Gladstone,' she wrote. The government, she believed, was full of dangerous

Republicans and Radicals (who called for drastic political and social change) and none worse than the Prime Minister.

Gladstone's attitude to the Empire was even more objectionable – he didn't seem to understand how important the Empire was, or how, when the honour of the Empire was at stake, action must be taken. 'Mr Gladstone cares little for and understands still less foreign affairs,' she wrote to Vicky.

She was outraged when Gladstone delayed in sending help to a British general, General Gordon, who was being besieged in the Sudan. As a result, Gordon was speared to death and his head was cut off and hung on a tree for three days. Of course Gladstone was to blame and she made sure he knew it.

'The Queen feels much aggrieved and annoyed,' wrote Victoria, 'She was never listened to, or her advice followed, and all she foretold invariably happened and what she urged was done when too late! It is dreadful for her to see how we are going downhill, and to be unable to prevent the humiliation of this country.'

When, in June 1885, Gladstone offered to resign (the Liberals were quarrelling among themselves), the

Queen, who was at Balmoral, breathed a sigh of relief. But she had no desire at all to leave Scotland, where she always spent June, and return to London in order to accept Gladstone's resignation and to see the new Tory Prime Minister, Lord Salisbury. Really, it was most inconvenient that political crises should develop when she was enjoying her holiday. 'The Queen is a lady nearer 70 than 60… and is quite unable to rush about as a younger person and a man could do,' she wrote crossly to Gladstone. But return she must.

When Gladstone came to Windsor, to deliver his seals of office, she refused to shake hands. His tall, gaunt figure, with his tufts of white hair and burning eyes, stood before her short, round one and bowed low. 'May I be permitted to kiss your hand, Ma'am?' he asked. Gazing somewhere over his shoulder, the Queen held out the merest tips of her fingers and with that Gladstone had to be content. She had not seen the back of him however, for Gladstone became Prime Minister not just once more, but twice. She never came to like the 'half-crazy old man' any better.

The last few years had brought death and loss for the Queen. December 14th, the anniversary of

Albert's death, was always a dark day. In 1878 it became even more so. That morning, as always, the Queen got up and went to the Blue Room to pray and remember Albert. As she was sitting at breakfast, John Brown came in with a telegram – her daughter Princess Alice, who had nursed her father so faithfully, had died on the very same day (she had caught diphtheria from her young son). Alice was the first child the Queen had lost, which, considering how many children died in the 19th century, was remarkable. Six years later she would lose another, Leopold, who finally succumbed to haemophilia.

In 1881 Disraeli also died (when he was asked if he'd like the Queen to visit him he declined, saying, 'No, it is better not. She will only ask me to send a message to Albert'). The Queen sent a wreath of primroses to be put on his coffin. And two years later it was the turn of John Brown himself, the Queen's 'strong arm'.

Although she had become more philosophical about death over the years, this was an awful blow. Brown, she wrote to Vicky, was 'my dearest best friend to whom I could speak quite openly… He protected me so, was so powerful and strong – I felt so safe.' In fact she was literally prostrated with grief and lost the use of her legs. A masseuse, known as 'the Rubber', came from France to try and rub some life back into the royal limbs. For the rest of her life the Queen walked with a stick, or used a wheelchair and, for outdoors, a pony cart.

Then, in 1887, Vicky's husband Fritz was diagnosed with cancer. It seemed that people younger than the Queen were dying all around her. Yet here was she about to celebrate her Golden Jubilee.

CHAPTER THIRTEEN

On June 20th 1887 the Queen woke to a beautiful morning – 'queen's weather' as usual. 'The day has come and I am alone, though surrounded by many dear children... 50 years today since I came to the Throne!' she wrote.

Jubilee preparations, mostly organised by the Prince of Wales, who loved a celebration, had been in full swing since the beginning of the year. On New Year's day, the Prince had presented his mother with a special Jubilee present – an inkstand in the shape of a crown, 'which opens and on the inside there is a head of me,' wrote the Queen happily. It was the first of hundreds of gifts, which poured in from all over the Empire.

Prisoners, from Britain and the Empire, had been released from jail (though the Queen put her foot down about one man who had been sentenced for cruelty to animals, a crime which she particularly abhorred), Jubilee medals and coins had been made, invitations sent out, rehearsals conducted, telegrams read, commemorative buildings opened. It was Jubilee mania. Shops were bursting with Jubilee mugs, teapots, tea towels and wallpaper. Women could even buy musical bustles that played 'God Save the Queen' when you sat down. No one had ever seen anything like it.

On June 21st an open landau (carriage), flanked by the Indian cavalry, carried the Queen to Westminster Abbey, for a Thanksgiving Service. She had flatly refused to wear a crown for the occasion. No, she would wear a bonnet, a special bonnet decorated with lace and diamonds. At the sight of their bonneted sovereign, the vast crowds lining the streets broke into wild cheers and Her Majesty's face lit up in an enchanting smile.

Inside the Abbey, the congregation heard the roar of the crowds and hastily put away their newspapers and sandwich wrappings. Minutes later the Queen appeared in the doorway, leaning on her stick. As she walked slowly up the aisle, her thoughts, as always, turned to Albert – 'I sat alone (Oh! Without my beloved husband, for whom this would have been such a proud day!)' she wrote.

Afterwards it was back to the palace, where she gave Jubilee brooches to the ladies in her family and pins to the men. There followed a lunch, then a naval parade, then a grand dinner, for which the Queen donned her Jubilee dress, embroidered with silver roses, thistles and shamrocks (the national emblems of England, Scotland and Ireland). For the fireworks she took to her wheelchair 'half-dead with fatigue'.

The next day 30,000 poor children gathered in Hyde Park and were given a bun, milk and a Jubilee mug. Military bands played and the children sang 'God Save the Queen' ('somewhat out of tune' said Her Majesty). As a huge balloon rose into the air, a small girl cried, 'Look! There's Queen Victoria going up to Heaven!' And the celebrations went on for weeks, with garden parties and receptions and military reviews. All in boiling heat. The Queen was quite worn out. 'Never, never can I forget this brilliant year,' she wrote as 1887 ended.

The Jubilee year brought two new servants, from India. The Queen was rightly proud of the fact that she didn't have an ounce of 'race prejudice', as she called it, and she was absolutely delighted, unlike everybody else, with Abdul Karim and Mohammed Bukhsh. Whenever possible, Victoria liked to have breakfast outside, under a tent. There, wearing dark blue native costumes and white turbans, her Indian servants would stand behind her chair, while their royal mistress ate her boiled egg from a gold egg cup with a gold spoon.

No one could replace John Brown, but handsome Abdul Karim, with his dark eyes and silken beard, became a particular favourite. He cooked her curries and gave her lessons in Hindustani. Soon he was promoted to her Indian Secretary, known as the 'Munshi', even though he could barely read or write. Before long there were cottages for the Munshi at Osborne and Balmoral, his family were brought from India and he was allowed to have meals in the house-hold dining-room. None of this went down well with the household. They didn't trust the Munshi a bit (it was discovered, for example, that the Munshi's father was not, as he claimed, a distinguished doctor, but merely a humble apothecary in a prison); he had impossible airs and graces and far too much influence with the Queen. Where would it end?

In the Queen's eyes, however, the Munshi could do no wrong. Criticism of him made her furious – it was hurtful to the 'poor Munshi's sensitive feelings' and it was simply prejudice. When her household said they would have to resign if she insisted on taking the Munshi to France with her, she lost her temper and swept everything off her desk onto the floor. She absolutely refused to send him back to India.

CHAPTER FOURTEEN

On September 23rd 1896 the Queen wrote, 'Today is the day on which I have reigned longer by a day than any English sovereign.' The following year, 1897, she celebrated her Diamond Jubilee.

By now the 78-year-old Queen was a grandmother and great-grandmother many times over (she had 37 great grandchildren by the time she died). For much of the time she was surrounded by family. She was extremely fond of the grandchildren and much less strict than she had been with her own children. And they were just as fond of 'Gangan' as they called her. They realised that if they were shy, so too was she. They recognised something child-like in the Queen.

She liked arranging treats. When the grandchildren

came to stay, she laid on performing bears, Punch and Judy, and, once, Buffalo Bill. Every grandchild on his or her tenth birthday would be given a gold watch. When angry, though, 'Gangan' could be terrifying and offences such as talking in church were instantly punished. So too was a granddaughter who, sick of boring nursery meals of mutton and rice pudding, said as her grace, 'Thank God for my dull dinner.'

The Queen's days followed the same pattern – breakfast, a morning outing in her pony cart, luncheon, an afternoon drive in the carriage, then tea and dinner. After dinner there were sometimes theatrical performances put on by the royal family and the household (occasionally professional actors were brought in). The Queen greatly enjoyed these – she would sit in an armchair, with a footstool and a small table for her fan, opera-glasses and programme, and lead the applause, tapping her hand with the fan. She had an irritating habit of explaining the plot to her neighbour, in a piercing whisper, while the play was going on.

Mealtimes, however, could be terribly dreary. The room was always freezing cold. The servants were often drunk. Guests would wait hopefully for the Queen to speak and sometimes, if she was sunk in gloom, she hardly spoke at all and merely shovelled food into her mouth. If someone dared tell a joke or a story that wasn't considered quite proper, the speaker would find him- or herself withered beneath the royal glare – the eyes would narrow, the corners of the mouth would droop and the dreaded words would be uttered, 'We are not amused.'

But more often than not Victoria *was* amused. When one of her great grandsons tried to pull her out of her chair after lunch and, finding he couldn't, ordered the Munshi: 'Man, pull it!', his great grand-mother laughed till tears ran down her cheeks. She was equally amused when, after a grandson wrote to her from school asking for more pocket money and she wrote back refusing, he replied saying it didn't matter as he'd already sold her letter of refusal for 30 shillings.

Yet the Queen was feeling her age. She slept badly. She was very lame. She suffered from indigestion, but still couldn't resist large helpings of roast beef and ice cream. Her eyesight was now so bad that documents had to be read to her by her daughter

Princess Beatrice (only in 1899 did she agree to wear glasses). Her country, however, was facing a struggle which needed its Queen to see it through. The Boer War broke out (for the second time) in South Africa in October 1899.

For Britain, the Boer War was more about greed than honour. It was fought over a part of South Africa called the Transvaal. The Transvaal had once been a British colony, but since 1881 it had been more or less independent and under the control of the Boers, who were originally from Holland and had settled in the Transvaal long before the British arrived. The British wanted the Transvaal back, especially since gold had been discovered there, while the Boers understandably felt threatened by the British. The result was war.

It turned into a long and bitter conflict, where thousands died quite unnecessarily. As far as the Queen was concerned, however, her job was not to ask questions, but to encourage her troops and lift the spirits of her subjects. When one week the British suffered one defeat after another – it was called 'Black Week' – she refused to be downcast and told the Prime Minister, Lord Salisbury, firmly: 'Please understand that there is no one depressed in this house; we are not interested in the possibilities of defeat; they do not exist.'

She visited hospitals, she reviewed troops, she knitted scarves, she presented medals and, sometimes, the V.C. (Victoria Cross) to returning soldiers. On the Queen's order, 100,000 tins of chocolate were sent to South Africa. These were so highly prized that some men refused to eat the chocolate; one claimed his tin had stopped a bullet and saved his life. When there was some good news the Queen drove in triumph through the streets of London and the crowds went wild with joy.

In May, five days before Victoria's 81st birthday, the town of Mafeking, which had been besieged by the Boers, was liberated and a group of boys from Eton school gathered outside Windsor Castle to sing patriotic songs. Looking up, they saw the Queen leaning out of a window, graciously calling 'Thank you, thank you!', as the brown arm of an Indian servant reached out with a large whisky. The worst of the war was over, though it was 1906 before peace was finally made.

Four thousand telegrams poured in for the Queen's

birthday. But the Boer War seemed to have drained away her energy. Her famous appetite shrank to nothing. She nodded off all the time. And sad news came from every side. In 1900 her son Alfred ('Affie') died. So, soon after, did one of her favourite grandsons. She had already lost three sons-in-law. In Germany her beloved daughter Vicky was dying, painfully and wretchedly, of cancer. The end was drawing in for Victoria too.

Christmas of 1900 was spent at Osborne, but it was not a happy one for the Queen. 'Another year begun, and I am feeling so weak and unwell that I enter upon it sadly,' she wrote on New Year's day. On January 18th her doctor, Sir James Reid, decided her children should be summoned. They hurried to Osborne. Her grandson, the German Kaiser, asked permission to come too. The Kaiser's bad behaviour had often made his grandmother furious, but permission was granted. Children and grandchildren stood around the Queen's bed and, whenever she seemed on the point of slipping away, called out their names. She opened her eyes, saw her eldest son and held out her arms to him, murmuring: 'Bertie...' It was the last word she spoke.

On January 22nd, at 6.30 p.m, she died.

When the announcement came, journalists bicycled furiously down the hill from Osborne to Cowes, in a race for the telephone. 'Queen dead! Queen dead!' came the cry, as they flashed past like crows, black coat tails flying in the wind. As the news spread across the country, people gathered in silent groups in the streets, gazing at each other in stunned bewilderment. For most of them Victoria was the only sovereign they'd ever known. She was like a mother. She had become an institution, a legend. She had seemed invincible – and now she was gone.

For ten days the Queen's body lay in state at Osborne. She wore a white dress, sprinkled with spring flowers, and her face was covered by her wedding veil. As she had requested, a number of objects, including Albert's dressing-gown and a photograph of John Brown (this to be placed in her left hand), were put in her coffin. On February 1st the coffin was taken on a yacht to the mainland and then by train to London. The blinds of the train were lowered, and people knelt in the fields as it steamed slowly past.

The Queen had always taken a keen interest in

funerals, including those of her dogs. So it's no surprise that she left detailed instructions for her own – it was to be military and, unusually, it was to be white (Victoria disliked black funerals – so unnecessarily gloomy, she thought). For the funeral procession the streets of London were hung with purple cashmere and white satin bows. The tiny coffin was carried on a gun carriage, pulled by eight white horses. Behind it rode Bertie, the new King, known as Edward VII, and the Kaiser. People stood watching in the biting February cold, dressed in black, their heads uncovered. Only the roll of drums, the hollow clip-clop of the horses' hooves and the rattle of swords broke the silence.

From London the coffin proceeded to Windsor, where there was a slight hitch when the horses' traces broke. A guard of sailors took over and dragged the gun carriage, by hand, to St George's Chapel. Three days later the coffin was taken to the Mausoleum at Frogmore. There the royal family filed past looking down into the grave where Victoria and Albert now lay side by side. In death, the Queen was finally reunited with the husband she had loved and mourned for 40 years. But for Victorians it was the end of an era. Without their dumpy, dependable little Queen, they were cut adrift into the unknown waters of the 20th century.

KEY DATES

1819 – Victoria is born in Kensington Palace.

1820 – Victoria's father, the Duke of Kent, dies of pneumonia.

1820 – George III dies and one of Victoria's uncles, the Prince Regent, becomes George IV.

1830 – George IV dies and another uncle, the Duke of Clarence, becomes William IV.

1836 – Victoria's seventeenth birthday. She meets her future husband Albert for the first time.

1837 – King William IV dies, and Victoria becomes Queen at the age of eighteen.

1839 – Queen Victoria proposes to Albert.

1840 – She and Albert get married.

1840 – She gives birth to her first child, a daughter, Vicky.

1841 – She gives birth to a son, Bertie.

1843 – She gives birth to Alice.

1843 – She and Albert buy Osborne House on the Isle of Wight.

1844 – She gives birth to Alfred.

1846 – She gives birth to Helena.

1848 – And Louise.

1848 – The French King, Louis Philippe, abdicates after anti-royalist rebellions in France. Queen Victoria becomes worried about the growing support for Republicanism in Europe.

1850 – Queen Victoria gives birth to Arthur.

1851 – The Queen opens the Great Exhibition in Hyde Park.

1853 – She gives birth to Leopold.

1854 – The Crimean War begins – the first war of her reign.

1857 – Victoria gives birth to Beatrice.

1857 – The Indian Army rises up against the British. India is taken out of the control of the East India Company and put under the direct rule of the Queen.

1861 – Queen Victoria's mother, the Duchess of Kent, dies.

1861 – Her husband Albert dies, and the Queen goes into deep mourning.

1863 – Queen Victoria's eldest son, Bertie, marries Princess Alexandra.

1864 – Queen Victoria takes up riding again, accompanied by her loyal servant John Brown.

1866 – She agrees to open parliament for the first time since Albert's death.

1876 – She becomes Empress of India.

1878 – Her daughter Princess Alice dies.

1883 – Her favourite servant John Brown dies.

1884 – Her son Leopold dies.

1899 – The Boer War breaks out in South Africa.

1900 – Queen Victoria's son Alfred dies.

1901 – Queen Victoria dies.

Kate Hubbard is the author of *A Material Girl: Bess of Hardwick* (Short Books 2001), and *Charlotte Brontë, The Girl who Turned her Life into a Book*, another in the **WHO WAS...** children's biography series. She lives in London and Dorset.

Dear Reader,

No matter how old you are, good books always leave you wanting to know more. If you have any questions you would like to ask the author, **Kate Hubbard,** about **Queen Victoria** please write to us at: SHORT BOOKS 15 Highbury Terrace, London N5 1UP.

If you enjoyed this title, then you would probably enjoy others in the series. Why not click on our website for more information and see what the teachers are being told? **www.theshortbookco.com**

All the books in the WHO WAS... series are available from TBS, Distribution Centre, Colchester Road, Frating Green, Colchester, Essex CO7 7DW (Tel: 01206 255800), at £4.99 + P&P.

OTHER TITLES IN THE **WHO WAS...** SERIES:

WHO WAS... Admiral Nelson
The Sailor Who Dared All to Win
Sam Llewellyn
1-904095-65-8

No one ever imagined that a weak skinny boy like Horatio Nelson would be able to survive the hardships of life at sea. But he did. In fact he grew up to become a great naval hero, the man who saved Britain from invasion by the dreaded Napoleon.

Nelson was someone who always did things his own way. He lost an eye and an arm in battle, but never let that hold him back. He was brilliant on ships, clumsy on land, ferocious in battle, knew fear but overcame it, and never, never took no for an answer.

This is his story.

WHO WAS... David Livingstone
The Legendary Explorer
Amanda Mitchison
1-904095-84-4

Born a poor Glasgow cotton-mill worker, David grew up
to become a great explorer and hero of his time.

This is his incredible story. The tough man of Victorian
Britain would stop at nothing in his determination to be
the first white man to explore Afirca, even if it meant
dragging his wife and children along with him.

He trekked hundreds of miles through dangerous terri-
tory, braving terrible illness and pain, and was attacked
by cannibals, rampaging lions and killer ants...

WHO WAS... Anne Boleyn
The Queen Who Lost her Head
Laura Beatty
1-904095-78-X

For Anne Boleyn, King Henry VIII threw away his wife, out-raged his people, chucked his religion, and drove his best friend to death.

What does it take to drive a King this crazy?
Was she a witch? An enchantress? Whatever she was,
Anne turned Tudor England upside-down and shook it.
And everyone was talking about her...

But Anne lived dangerously. And when she could
not give the King the one thing he wanted – a son –
his love went out like a light. The consequences for Anne
were deadly...

WHO WAS... Alexander Selkirk
Survivor on a Desert Island
Amanda Mitchison
1-904095-79-8

On the beach stood a wild thing waving its arms and hollering. The thing had the shape of a man, but it was all covered in fur, like a Barbary ape. What was it? A new kind of animal? A monster?

It was Alexander Selkirk, Scottish mariner and adventurer, thrilled to be rescued by passing sailors after four years alone on a Pacific island. This is the story of how Selkirk came to be stranded on the island and how he survived, the story of...
THE REAL ROBINSON CRUSOE.

WHO WAS... Ada Lovelace
Computer Wizard of Victorian England
Lucy Lethbridge
1-904095-76-3

Daughter of the famous poet Lord Byron, Ada Lovelace
was a child prodigy. Brilliant at maths, she read numbers
like most people read words.

In 1834 she came to the attention of Charles Babbage, a
scientist and techno0whizz who had just built an amaz-
ing new 'THINKING MACHINE'. Ada and Mr
Babbage made a perfect partnership, which produced the
most important invention of the modern world – THE
COMPUTER!

*WINNER OF THE BLUE PETER
BOOK AWARD 2002!*

WHO WAS... Charlotte Brontë
The Girl Who Turned her Life into a Book
Kate Hubbard
1-904095-80-1

Of the famous Bronte siblings, Charlotte, the eldest, was the survivor. At eight, she was packed off to a boarding school so harsh that it killed two of her sisters. Her adult years were equally haunted by tragedy.

But one thing kept Charlotte going: she had a secret talent for story-telling. This is the tale of a remarkable woman, who turned her own life into one of the world's greatest classic novels, *Jane Eyre*.

WHO WAS... Ned Kelly
Gangster Hero of the Australian Outback
Charlie Boxer
1-904095-61-5

Born into a family of Irish settlers in Australia, Ned
Kelly grew up bad. Cattle and horse thieving led him
into regular dust-ups with the law. Then, at 23, while on
the run, he shot a policeman dead.

For two years Ned and his gang of outlaws hid in the
outback, making a mockery of all attempts to catch
them. This is the story of how a bushranger declared
war on his country's police and became a great
national hero.

WHO WAS... Florence Nightingale
The Lady with the Lamp
Charlotte Moore
1-904095-83-6

Even as a little girl, Florence Nightingale knew
she was different. Unlike the rest of her family, she
wasn't interested in fancy clothes or grand parties.
She knew God wanted her to do something different,
something important... but what?

In 1854, shocking everyone, she set off to help
save the thousands of British soldiers injured in the
disastrous Crimean war. Nothing could have prepared
her for the horror of the army hospital, where
soldiers writhed in agony as rats scuttled around
them on the blood-stained floor.

But Florence set to work, and became the greatest
nurse the world had ever seen...

Emily Davison
The girl who gave her life for her cause
Claudia FitzHerbert
1-904095-66-6

Sam Johnson
The wonderful word doctor
Andrew Billen
1-904095-77-1

Annie Oakley
Sharpshooter of the Wild West
Lucy Lethbridge
1-904095-60-7

Madame Tussaud
Waxwork queen of the French Revolution
Tony Thorne
1-904095-85-2

Nelson Mandela
The prisoner who gave the world hope
Adrian Hadland
1-904095-86-0

The Bloody Baron
Evil invader of the East
Nick Middleton
1-904095-87-9